WAVES OF INSPIRATIONAL QUOTES

ON

THE WORD

By

Sekudo Michael Ajiboye

PUBLICATION

This piece is the original work of the author. No part of this book is permitted to be reproduced or used for publication, intellectual discuss without permission and reference to the author of this book.

ISBN: 978-978-58020-7-8

Type Setting/Compilation:

Daniel Agboje

Tel: 07035730526, 08067268410
Email: dan4exploit@gmail.com
Website: idealtech.com.ng
Port Harcourt, Nigeria.

Publisher : Miketojane Ltd.

Tel: 08033688772, 08057314120
Email : miketojane.info@gmail.com

APPRECIATION

All gratitude goes to God who is the Giver of wisdom and understanding, for the inspiration given to put this together and for this piece to be a blessing to others. My appreciation goes to my lovely wife and my children for sacrificing their time and comfort at the moment of working on this book.

I wish to sincerely appreciate the impacts of my spiritual fathers: Bishop David Oyedepo and Bishop David Abioye, my mentors, seniors, leaders, friends, well wishers and colleagues in the work of the ministry for the inspiration, words of encouragement and support received towards this publication.

I will not forget to acknowledge the effort of my graphic designer Daniel Agboje, who typed, compiled and designed the content of this book. My sincere appreciation goes to the CEO of MIKETOJANE PRINTING AND PUBLISHING LIMITED for editing, professional packaging and publishing of the book.

INTRODUCTION

Inspirations are products of divine revelations delivered by the Spirit of God to man; documented to impact and transform others. This publication is a product of such Revelational experience. Be blessed as you go through this piece of work.

SEKUDO MICHAEL AJIBOYE
@michaelajiboye4@gmail.com
@msekudo(Twitter)
michaelajiboyesekudo(Instagram)
www.d-blossomsupernaturalhighways.org.ng

" EVERY CAPSULE(SCRIPTURE) OF THE WORD THAT SETTLES IN A MAN, INCREASES HIS CAPACITY FOR CONSTANT DOMINION."

" THE BEST DESCRIPTION OF GOD IS FOUND ON
THE PAGES OF THE SCRIPTURES."

" WHEN A MAN IS GIVEN TO THE WORD, HE HAS
SECURED THE CURRENCY FOR CONSTANT
RELEVANCE IN ALL ENDEAVORS."

" WHEN THE CONSCIENCE OF MAN IS REGULATED BY THE POWER OF THE WORD, HE'S EMPOWERED TO DEREGULATE THE WORLD OF INIQUITY."

" THE REVELATION OF THE WORD, IS THE CURE
FOR ALL SPIRITUAL BLINDNESS."

" THE WORD OF GOD, REMAINS THE ONE AND ONLY ETERNAL BOOK, THAT REBUKES WITHOUT COMPROMISES, YET RE-BUILDS WITH ABSOLUTE MERCY, IF MAN EMBRACES GENUINE REPENTANCE IN GOD."

" GOD IS ALWAYS AVAILABLE THROUGH HIS WORD, BUT MAY NOT BE ACCESSIBLE, UNTIL THE SPIRIT OF MAN, UNDERSTAND THE VOICE OF GOD THROUGH HIS WORD."

" THE BEST DEFINITION OF PEACE, IN THE MIDST
OF STORMS, IS BEST DEFINED BY THE ABSOLUTE
QUIETNESS IN THE HEART OF MAN BIRTH BY THE
ENCOUNTER WITH THE WORD OF GOD."

" NOTHING KEEPS THE WORD OF GOD AFLAME
IN THE HEART OF MAN, LIKE THE SPIRIT OF GOD."

" THE STRENGTH OF YOUR SPIRIT MAN IS
ROOTED IN THE SPIRIT OF THE WORD AT WORK
IN YOUR HEART."

" IT IS THE WORD THAT HELPS A MAN TO SEE
WHAT GOD SEES, THINK THE WAY GOD THINKS,
ACT THE WAY GOD ACTS, AND LIVE THE WAY
GOD LIVES."

" WHEN THE WORD IS AT WORK IN THE HEART
OF A MAN, HIS LIFE GAINS A WORTH WITH GOD."

" THE TRUE PROOF OF SPIRITUALITY, IS THE FRUIT
OF THE WORD AT WORK IN THE LIFE OF A
BELIEVER."

" ONLY THROUGH THE WORD, CAN THE TREASURES OF LIFE BECOME ACCESSIBLE TO TERMINATE THE PRESSURES OF LIFE."

" THE WORD IS GOD'S CONSTITUTION HANDED OVER TO MAN TO ENFORCE THE LIFESTYLE OF HEAVEN ON EARTH."

" THE WORD IS GOD, ...AN EXPRESSION OF THE
LIFESTYLE OF GOD, ...HIS WAYS , WEIGHT,
THOUGHT AND ACTIONS."

" IT IS THE PROPHETIC DIMENSION OF THE WORD
THAT YOU DISCOVER, UNDERSTAND, BELIEVE,
AND PRACTICE THAT DETERMINES THE
MIRACULOUS YOU WILL ENJOY AND
EXPERIENCE."

" IT IS BETTER TO BE DRIVEN , DRUNK, SOAKED
WITH A SINGLE REVELATION OF THE WORD AND
TAKE PERPETUAL DOMINION THAN TO BE
LOADED WITH HALF BAKED REVELATION AND BE
STRANDED OR CONFUSED IN LIFE."

" ANYTIME YOU HEAR 'THUS SAYS THE LORD', ALL
TOUGH CASES GIVES WAY WITH EASE."

" UNTIL YOU STAY AWAKE WITH THE WORD, YOU
CAN'T COMMAND A WEIGHT AMONG MEN."

" SCRIPTURAL MEDITATION, IS THE SPIRITUAL
MEDICATION FOR ALL SPIRITUAL FRUSTRATION
AND ILLNESSES."

"THE WORD IS THE MYSTERIES OF GOD CLASSIFIED OR DIVIDED INTO VERSES. "

"THE WORD IS THE VOICE OF GOD IN A WRITTEN
FORM. "

"THE ' WORD' IS THE POWER OF GOD EXPRESSED
IN LETTERS."

"THE WORD IS THE ONLY BOOK THAT THE
AUTHOR IS ALWAYS AVAILABLE TO TALK WITH,
WHEN READING,THOUGH INVISIBLE."

" THE WORD IS THE SPIRIT OF GOD INTERACTING
WITH MAN ON THE PAGES OF PAPER."

" THE WORD IS THE ETERNAL SECRET OF HEAVEN,
HIDDEN IN THE PAGES OF THE BIBLE, ONLY THE
SPIRITUAL CAN ACCESS IT."

" WHEN THE VOICE OF THE WORD SOUNDS IN THE SPIRIT OF A MAN, HE'S EMPOWERED TO CONQUER ALL IMPOSSIBILITIES IN THE PHYSICAL."

" IT IS THE VOICE OF THE WORD THAT COORDINATES THE ATTENTION OF ALL CREATURES TOWARDS THE CREATOR...WHEN GOD SPEAKS, EVERYTHING HEARS AND OBEY."

" THE SIMPLEST WAY TO INTERACT AND
UNDERSTAND GOD IS THROUGH THE SIMPLIFIED
WORD OF GOD."

" IT IS THE WORD AT WORK IN THE LIFE OF A
MAN, THAT MAKE HIM GAIN RESEMBLANCE
WITH GOD."

" THE WORD OF GOD IS THE RE-ACTIVATING
POWER FOR A DEAD CONSCIENCE."

" OUR COMPANIONSHIP WITH GOD, IS ENHANCED BY OUR CLOSENESS TO THE WORD OF GOD."

" ANYTIME YOU GET IT RIGHT WITH THE WORD,
YOU WILL ALWAYS GET IT RIGHT WITH GOD."

" THE COMMUNICATION NETWORK BETWEEN
THE CONSCIENCE OF MAN AND THE CONSENT OF
GOD, IS THE WORD OF GOD BIRTH IN THE HEART
OF MAN."

" THE WORD OF GOD REMAINS THE ETERNAL
CURE TO THE SPIRITUAL AND MENTAL
IGNORANCE OF MAN."

" WHEN YOUR LIFE RUNS DRY OF THE WORD,
YOU WANDER IN LIFE...AND RUN EMPTY OF
GOD."

" WHEN THE WORD OF GOD, GETS HOLD OF
YOUR HEART, THE WORLD LOSES ITS GRIP OVER
YOUR LIFE.."

" ONLY THOSE WHO SETTLES WITH THE WORD,
WILL HAVE A SETTLED DESTINY...THE SETTLED
WORD , IS WHAT SETTLES YOUR WORLD."

" ANYTIME YOU SUBMIT TO SATANIC
NEGOTIATION ON ANY COVENANT DEMAND,
YOU BECOME RELEGATED SPIRITUALLY."

" THE MORE YOU 'EAT' THE WORD, THE BETTER
YOU DECIPATE THE HEAT' OF LIFE."

" THE WORD, IS AN EXPRESSION OF THE VARIOUS
PARTS THAT MAKE UP THE COMPONENTS OF
GOD'S PERSONALITY."

" IT IS THE SPIRIT OF THE WORD THAT KEEPS A
MAN FLYING IN THE SAME ALTITUDE WITH GOD."

" IT IS BETTER TO KNOW ONE SCRIPTURE AND
HAVE A FUTURE, THAN TO KNOW TOO MANY
SCRIPTURES AND BE RUPTURE IN LIFE."

" IT IS CHEAPER TO READ THE WORD, BUT IS FAR
BETTER TO KEEP THE WORD."

" UNTIL YOUR CHALLENGES ARE ADDRESSED
FROM THE 'WORD APPROACH' , YOU MAY NOT
RECOVER FROM THE WORLD REPROACH."

" WHAT GIVES THE SUPERNATURAL MOTION
FOR STRANGE MANIFESTATION , IS THE WEIGHT
OF A SPOKEN WORD."

" EVERY REVELATION YOU CATCH FROM THE WORD...AND PRACTICE...GUARANTEES AN ELEVATION AMONG MEN."

" UNTIL YOU STAND TALL IN THE WORD, YOU
CAN'T STAND STRONG AGAINST THE WORLD."

" UNTIL YOU WAIT ON THE WORD, YOU WILL
WASTE WAY IN NO TIME."